table of contents

mashed rutabagas and potatoes

Makes 8 servings

- 2 pounds rutabagas, peeled and cut into ½-inch pieces
- 1 pound potatoes, peeled and cut into ½-inch pieces
- ½ cup milk
- ½ teaspoon ground nutmeg
- 2 tablespoons chopped fresh Italian parsley
  Sprig fresh Italian parsley (optional)

1. Place rutabagas and potatoes in **CROCK-POT**® slow cooker; add enough water to cover vegetables. Cover; cook on LOW 6 hours or on HIGH 3 hours. Remove vegetables to large bowl using slotted spoon. Discard cooking liquid.

2. Mash vegetables with potato masher. Add milk, nutmeg and chopped parsley; stir until smooth. Garnish with parsley sprigs.

cheesy corn and peppers

Makes 8 servings

- 2 pounds frozen corn
- 2 poblano peppers, chopped
- 2 tablespoons butter, cubed
- 1 teaspoon salt
- ½ teaspoon ground cumin
- ¼ teaspoon black pepper
- 3 ounces cream cheese, cubed
- 1 cup (4 ounces) shredded sharp Cheddar cheese

1. Coat inside of **CROCK-POT**® slow cooker with nonstick cooking spray. Combine corn, poblano peppers, butter, salt, cumin and black pepper in **CROCK-POT**® slow cooker. Cover; cook on HIGH 2 hours.

2. Stir in cheeses. Cover; cook on HIGH 15 minutes or until cheeses are melted.

mashed rutabagas and potatoes

orange-spice glazed carrots

Makes 6 servings

- 1 package (32 ounces) baby carrots
- ½ cup packed light brown sugar
- ½ cup orange juice
- 1 tablespoon unsalted butter
- ¾ teaspoon ground cinnamon
- ¼ teaspoon ground nutmeg
- ¼ cup cold water
- 2 tablespoons cornstarch

1. Combine carrots, brown sugar, orange juice, butter, cinnamon and nutmeg in **CROCK-POT**® slow cooker. Cover; cook on LOW 3½ to 4 hours. Remove carrots to large serving bowl using slotted spoon.

2. Turn **CROCK-POT**® slow cooker to HIGH. Stir water into cornstarch in small bowl until smooth; whisk into cooking liquid. Cover; cook on HIGH 15 minutes or until thickened. Spoon sauce evenly over carrots.

creamy curried spinach

Makes 6 to 8 servings

- 3 packages (10 ounces *each*) frozen spinach, thawed
- 1 onion, chopped
- 4 teaspoons minced garlic
- 2 tablespoons curry powder
- 2 tablespoons butter, melted
- ¼ cup chicken broth
- ¼ cup whipping cream
- 1 teaspoon lemon juice

Combine spinach, onion, garlic, curry powder, butter and broth in **CROCK-POT**® slow cooker; stir to blend. Cover; cook on LOW 3 to 4 hours or on HIGH 2 hours. Stir in cream and lemon juice during last 30 minutes of cooking.

orange-spice glazed carrots

roasted summer squash with pine nuts and romano cheese

Makes 6 to 8 servings

- 2 tablespoons olive oil
- ½ cup chopped yellow onion
- 1 medium red bell pepper, chopped
- 1 clove garlic, minced
- 3 medium zucchini, cut into ½-inch slices
- 3 medium summer squash, cut into ½-inch slices
- ½ cup chopped pine nuts
- ⅓ cup grated Romano cheese
- 1 teaspoon Italian seasoning
- 1 teaspoon salt
- ¼ teaspoon black pepper
- 1 tablespoon unsalted butter, cubed
- Sprigs fresh basil (optional)

1. Heat oil in large skillet over medium-high heat. Add onion, bell pepper and garlic; cook and stir 10 minutes or until onion is translucent and soft. Remove to **CROCK-POT®** slow cooker. Add zucchini and summer squash; toss lightly.

2. Combine pine nuts, cheese, Italian seasoning, salt and black pepper in small bowl. Fold half of cheese mixture into squash. Sprinkle remaining cheese mixture on top. Dot with butter. Cover; cook on LOW 4 to 6 hours. Garnish with basil.

red cabbage and apples

Makes 6 servings

  1 small head red cabbage, cored and thinly sliced
  1 large apple, peeled and grated
  ¾ cup sugar
  ½ cup red wine vinegar
  1 teaspoon ground cloves
  ½ cup bacon, crisp-cooked and crumbled (optional)
     Fresh apple slices (optional)

Combine cabbage, grated apple, sugar, vinegar and cloves in **CROCK-POT**® slow cooker; stir to blend. Cover; cook on HIGH 6 hours, stirring halfway through cooking time. Sprinkle with bacon, if desired. Garnish with apple slices.

rustic cheddar mashed potatoes

Makes 8 servings

  2 pounds russet potatoes, diced
  1 cup water
  2 tablespoons unsalted butter, cubed
  ¾ cup milk
  ¾ teaspoon salt
  ½ teaspoon black pepper
  ½ cup finely chopped green onions
  2 tablespoons shredded Cheddar cheese

1. Combine potatoes, water and butter in **CROCK-POT**® slow cooker. Cover; cook on LOW 6 hours or on HIGH 3 hours. Remove potatoes to large bowl using slotted spoon.

2. Beat potatoes with electric mixer at medium speed 2 to 3 minutes or until well blended. Add milk, salt and pepper; beat 2 minutes or until well blended.

3. Stir in green onions and cheese. Cover; let stand 15 minutes or until cheese is melted.

red cabbage and apples

slow-cooked succotash

Makes 8 servings

- 2 teaspoons canola oil
- 1 cup diced onion
- 1 cup diced green bell pepper
- 1 cup diced celery
- 1 teaspoon paprika
- 1½ cups frozen corn
- 1½ cups frozen lima beans
- 1 cup canned diced tomatoes
- 2 teaspoons dried parsley flakes *or* 1 tablespoon minced fresh Italian parsley
- ½ teaspoon salt
- ½ teaspoon black pepper

1. Heat oil in large skillet over medium heat. Add onion, bell pepper and celery; cook and stir 5 minutes or until vegetables are crisp-tender. Stir in paprika.

2. Stir onion mixture, corn, beans, tomatoes, parsley flakes, salt and black pepper into **CROCK-POT**® slow cooker. Cover; cook on LOW 6 to 8 hours or on HIGH 3 to 4 hours.

asian golden barley with cashews

Makes 4 servings

- 2 tablespoons olive oil
- 1 cup hulled barley, sorted
- 3 cups vegetable broth
- 1 cup chopped celery
- 1 medium green bell pepper, chopped
- 1 medium yellow onion, chopped
- 1 clove garlic, minced
- ¼ teaspoon black pepper
- 1 ounce finely chopped cashews

1. Heat large skillet over medium heat. Add oil and barley; cook and stir 10 minutes or until barley is slightly browned. Remove to **CROCK-POT**® slow cooker.

2. Add broth, celery, bell pepper, onion, garlic and black pepper; stir to blend. Cover; cook on LOW 4 to 5 hours or on HIGH 2 to 3 hours until liquid is absorbed. Top with cashews.

blue cheese potatoes

Makes 5 servings

- 2 pounds red potatoes, peeled and cut into ½-inch pieces
- 1¼ cups chopped green onions, divided
- 2 tablespoons olive oil, divided
- 1 teaspoon dried basil
- ½ teaspoon salt
- ¼ teaspoon black pepper
- ½ cup crumbled blue cheese

1. Layer potatoes, 1 cup green onions, 1 tablespoon oil, basil, salt and pepper in **CROCK-POT**® slow cooker. Cover; cook on LOW 7 hours or on HIGH 4 hours.

2. Gently stir in cheese and remaining 1 tablespoon oil. Cover; cook on HIGH 5 minutes. Remove potatoes to large serving platter; top with remaining ¼ cup green onions.

asian golden barley with cashews

asparagus and cheese

Makes 4 to 6 servings

1½ pounds fresh asparagus, trimmed
2 cups crushed saltine crackers
1 can (10¾ ounces) condensed cream of asparagus soup, undiluted
1 can (10¾ ounces) condensed cream of chicken or cream of celery soup, undiluted
4 ounces American cheese, cut into cubes
⅔ cup slivered almonds
1 egg

Combine asparagus, crackers, soups, cheese, almonds and egg in **CROCK-POT**® slow cooker; stir to blend. Cover; cook on HIGH 3 to 3½ hours.

tarragon carrots in white wine

Makes 6 to 8 servings

8 medium carrots, cut into matchsticks
½ cup chicken broth
½ cup dry white wine
1 tablespoon lemon juice
1 tablespoon minced fresh tarragon
2 teaspoons finely chopped green onions
1½ teaspoons chopped fresh Italian parsley
1 clove garlic, minced
1 teaspoon salt
2 tablespoons melba toast, crushed
2 tablespoons cold water

1. Combine carrots, broth, wine, lemon juice, tarragon, green onions, parsley, garlic and salt in **CROCK-POT**® slow cooker; stir to blend. Cover; cook on LOW 2½ to 3 hours or on HIGH 1½ to 2 hours.

2. Dissolve toast crumbs in water in small bowl; add to carrots. Cover; cook on LOW 10 minutes or until thickened.

asparagus and cheese

mexican-style spinach

Makes 6 servings

3 packages (10 ounces *each*) frozen chopped spinach, thawed
1 tablespoon canola oil
1 onion, chopped
1 clove garlic, minced
2 Anaheim chiles, roasted, peeled and minced*
3 fresh tomatillos, roasted, husks removed and chopped**
6 tablespoons sour cream (optional)

To roast chiles, heat large heavy skillet over medium-high heat. Add chiles; cook and turn until blackened all over. Place chiles in brown paper bag 2 to 5 minutes. Remove chiles from bag; scrape off charred skin. Cut off top and pull out core. Slice lengthwise; scrape off veins and any remaining seeds with a knife.

**To roast tomatillos, heat large heavy skillet over medium heat. Add tomatillos with papery husks; cook 10 minutes or until husks are brown and interior flesh is soft. Remove and discard husks when cool enough to handle.*

1. Place spinach in **CROCK-POT**® slow cooker.

2. Heat oil in large skillet over medium heat. Add onion and garlic; cook and stir 5 minutes or until onion is tender. Add chiles and tomatillos; cook 3 to 4 minutes. Remove onion mixture to **CROCK-POT**® slow cooker.

3. Cover; cook on LOW 4 to 6 hours. Serve with sour cream, if desired.

orange-spiced sweet potatoes

Makes 8 servings

2 pounds sweet potatoes, diced

½ cup packed dark brown sugar

2 tablespoons unsalted butter, cubed

1 teaspoon ground cinnamon

½ teaspoon ground nutmeg

½ teaspoon grated orange peel

Juice of 1 medium orange

¼ teaspoon salt

1 teaspoon vanilla

Chopped toasted pecans (optional)*

To toast pecans, spread in single layer in small skillet. Cook and stir over medium heat 1 to 2 minutes or until nuts are lightly browned.

Combine potatoes, brown sugar, butter, cinnamon, nutmeg, orange peel, orange juice, salt and vanilla in **CROCK-POT**® slow cooker; stir to blend. Cover; cook on LOW 4 hours or on HIGH 2 hours. Sprinkle with pecans, if desired.

Tip: For a creamy variation, mash potatoes with a hand masher or electric mixer, and add ¼ cup milk or whipping cream for moist consistency. Sprinkle with cinnamon-sugar and toasted pecans.

green bean casserole

Makes 6 servings

2 packages (10 ounces *each*) frozen green beans
1 can (10¾ ounces) condensed cream of mushroom soup, undiluted
1 tablespoon chopped fresh Italian parsley
1 tablespoon chopped roasted red peppers
1 teaspoon dried sage
½ teaspoon salt
½ teaspoon black pepper
¼ teaspoon ground nutmeg
½ cup toasted slivered almonds*

*To toast almonds, spread in single layer in small skillet. Cook and stir over medium heat 1 to 2 minutes or until nuts are lightly browned.

Combine beans, soup, parsley, red peppers, sage, salt, black pepper and nutmeg in **CROCK-POT**® slow cooker; stir to blend. Cover; cook on LOW 3 to 4 hours. Sprinkle each serving with almonds.

fennel braised with tomato

Makes 6 servings

    2 bulbs fennel
    1 tablespoon olive oil
    1 onion, sliced
    1 clove garlic, sliced
    4 tomatoes, chopped
    ⅔ cup vegetable broth
    3 tablespoons dry white wine
    1 tablespoon chopped fresh marjoram *or* 1 teaspoon dried marjoram
    ¼ teaspoon salt
    ¼ teaspoon black pepper

1. Trim stems and bottoms from fennel bulbs, reserving green leafy tops for garnish. Cut each bulb lengthwise into four wedges.

2. Heat oil in large skillet over medium heat. Add fennel, onion and garlic; cook and stir 5 minutes or until onion is soft and translucent. Remove fennel mixture to **CROCK-POT**® slow cooker.

3. Add tomatoes, broth, wine, marjoram, salt and pepper; stir to blend. Cover; cook on LOW 2 to 3 hours or on HIGH 1 to 1½ hours. Garnish with reserved green leafy tops.

chunky ranch potatoes

Makes 8 servings

    3 pounds unpeeled red potatoes, quartered
    1 cup water
    ½ cup prepared ranch dressing
    ½ cup grated Parmesan or Cheddar cheese
    ¼ cup minced fresh chives

1. Place potatoes in **CROCK-POT**® slow cooker. Add water. Cover; cook on LOW 7 to 9 hours or on HIGH 4 to 6 hours.

2. Stir in ranch dressing, cheese and chives. Break up potatoes into large pieces.

fennel braised with tomato

cheesy cauliflower

Makes 8 to 10 servings

3 pounds cauliflower florets
¼ cup water
5 tablespoons unsalted butter
1 cup finely chopped onion
6 tablespoons all-purpose flour
¼ teaspoon dry mustard
2 cups milk
2 cups (8 ounces) shredded sharp Cheddar cheese
½ teaspoon salt
¼ teaspoon black pepper

1. Coat inside of **CROCK-POT**® slow cooker with nonstick cooking spray. Add cauliflower and water.

2. Melt butter in medium saucepan over medium-high heat. Add onion; cook 4 to 5 minutes or until slightly softened. Add flour and mustard; cook and stir 3 minutes or until well combined. Whisk in milk until smooth. Bring to a boil; cook 1 to 2 minutes or until thickened. Stir in cheese, salt and pepper; cook and stir until cheese is melted. Pour cheese mixture over top of cauliflower in **CROCK-POT**® slow cooker. Cover; cook on LOW 4 to 4½ hours.

confetti black beans

Makes 6 servings

  1 cup dried black beans, rinsed and sorted
  3 cups water
1½ teaspoons olive oil
  1 medium onion, chopped
  ¼ cup chopped red bell pepper
  ¼ cup chopped yellow bell pepper
  1 jalapeño pepper, finely chopped*
  1 large tomato, chopped
  ½ teaspoon salt
  ⅛ teaspoon black pepper
  2 cloves garlic, minced
  1 can (about 14 ounces) chicken broth
  1 whole bay leaf
     Hot pepper sauce (optional)

Jalapeño peppers can sting and irritate the skin, so wear rubber gloves when handling peppers and do not touch your eyes.

1. Place beans in large bowl and add enough cold water to cover by at least 2 inches. Soak 6 to 8 hours or overnight.** Drain beans; discard water.

2. Heat oil in large skillet over medium heat. Add onion, bell peppers and jalapeño pepper; cook and stir 5 minutes or until onion is tender. Add tomato, salt and black pepper; cook 5 minutes. Stir in garlic.

3. Place beans, broth and bay leaf in **CROCK-POT**® slow cooker. Add onion mixture. Cover; cook on LOW 7 to 8 hours or on HIGH 4½ to 5 hours. Remove and discard bay leaf. Serve with hot pepper sauce, if desired.

**To quick soak beans, place beans in large saucepan; cover with water. Bring to a boil over high heat. Boil 2 minutes. Remove from heat; let soak, covered, 1 hour.

french carrot medley

Makes 6 servings

 2 cups sliced carrots
 ¾ cup unsweetened orange juice
 1 can (4 ounces) sliced mushrooms, undrained
 4 stalks celery, sliced
 2 tablespoons chopped onion
 ½ teaspoon dried dill weed
  Salt and black pepper
 ¼ cup cold water
 2 teaspoons cornstarch

1. Combine carrots, orange juice, mushrooms, celery, onion, dill weed, salt and pepper in **CROCK-POT®** slow cooker; stir to blend. Cover; cook on LOW 3 to 4 hours or on HIGH 2 hours.

2. Stir water into cornstarch in small bowl until smooth; whisk into cooking liquid. Cover; cook on HIGH 15 minutes or until sauce is thickened. Spoon sauce over vegetable mixture before serving.

candied sweet potatoes

Makes 4 servings

 3 medium sweet potatoes (1½ to 2 pounds),
  sliced into ½-inch rounds
 ½ cup water
 ¼ cup (½ stick) butter, cubed
 ½ cup sugar
 1 tablespoon vanilla
 1 teaspoon nutmeg

Combine potatoes, water, butter, sugar, vanilla and nutmeg in **CROCK-POT®** slow cooker; stir to blend. Cover; cook on LOW 7 hours or on HIGH 4 hours.

french carrot medley

garlicky mustard greens

Makes 4 servings

- 2 pounds mustard greens
- 1 teaspoon olive oil
- 1 cup chopped onion
- 2 cloves garlic, minced
- ¾ cup chopped red bell pepper
- ½ cup chicken or vegetable broth
- 1 tablespoon cider vinegar
- 1 teaspoon sugar

1. Remove stems and any wilted leaves from greens. Stack several leaves; roll up. Cut crosswise into 1-inch slices. Repeat with remaining greens.

2. Heat oil in large saucepan over medium heat. Add onion and garlic; cook and stir 5 minutes or until onion is tender. Combine greens, onion mixture, pepper and broth in **CROCK-POT**® slow cooker; stir to blend. Cover; cook on LOW 3 to 4 hours or on HIGH 2 hours.

3. Combine vinegar and sugar in small bowl; stir until sugar is dissolved. Stir into cooked greens; serve immediately.

lemon-mint red potatoes

Makes 4 servings

- 2 pounds new red potatoes
- 3 tablespoons extra virgin olive oil
- 1 teaspoon salt
- ½ teaspoon Greek seasoning or dried oregano
- ¼ teaspoon garlic powder
- ¼ teaspoon black pepper
- 4 tablespoons chopped fresh mint, divided
- 2 tablespoons butter
- 2 tablespoons lemon juice
- 1 teaspoon grated lemon peel

1. Coat inside of **CROCK-POT**® slow cooker with nonstick cooking spray. Add potatoes and oil, stirring gently to coat. Sprinkle with salt, Greek seasoning, garlic powder and pepper. Cover; cook on LOW 7 hours or on HIGH 4 hours.

2. Stir in 2 tablespoons mint, butter, lemon juice and lemon peel until butter is completely melted. Cover; cook on HIGH 15 minutes. Sprinkle with remaining 2 tablespoons mint.

Tip: It's easy to prepare these potatoes ahead of time. Simply follow the recipe and then turn off the heat. Let it stand at room temperature for up to 2 hours. You may reheat or serve the potatoes at room temperature.

sensational side dishes

brussels sprouts with bacon, thyme and raisins

Makes 8 servings

2 pounds Brussels sprouts
1 cup chicken broth
⅔ cup golden raisins
2 thick slices applewood smoked bacon, chopped
2 tablespoons chopped fresh thyme

Trim ends from sprouts; cut in half lengthwise through core (or in quarters). Combine sprouts, broth, raisins, bacon and thyme in **CROCK-POT**® slow cooker; stir to blend. Cover; cook on LOW 3 to 4 hours.

lemon cauliflower

Makes 6 servings

1 tablespoon butter
3 cloves garlic, minced
2 tablespoons lemon juice
½ cup water
6 cups (about 1½ pounds) cauliflower florets
4 tablespoons chopped fresh Italian parsley, divided
½ teaspoon grated lemon peel
¼ cup grated Parmesan cheese
  Lemon slices (optional)

1. Heat butter in small saucepan over medium heat. Add garlic; cook and stir 2 to 3 minutes or until soft. Stir in lemon juice and water.

2. Combine garlic mixture, cauliflower, 1 tablespoon parsley and lemon peel in **CROCK-POT**® slow cooker; stir to blend. Cover; cook on LOW 4 hours.

3. Sprinkle with remaining 3 tablespoons parsley and cheese before serving. Garnish with lemon slices.

brussels sprouts with bacon,
thyme and raisins

chili barbecue beans

Makes 8 to 10 servings

 1 cup dried Great Northern beans, rinsed and sorted
 1 cup dried red beans or dried kidney beans, rinsed and sorted
 1 cup dried baby lima beans, rinsed and sorted
 3 cups water
 8 slices bacon, crisp-cooked and crumbled *or* 8 ounces smoked sausage, sliced
 ¼ cup packed brown sugar
 2 tablespoons minced onion
 2 cubes beef bouillon
 1 teaspoon dry mustard
 1 teaspoon chili powder
 1 teaspoon minced garlic
 ½ teaspoon black pepper
 ¼ teaspoon red pepper flakes
 2 whole bay leaves
 1 to 1½ cups barbecue sauce

1. Place beans in large bowl and add enough cold water to cover by at least 2 inches. Soak 6 to 8 hours or overnight.* Drain beans; discard water.

2. Combine soaked beans, 3 cups water, bacon, brown sugar, onion, bouillon cubes, mustard, chili powder, garlic, black pepper, red pepper flakes and bay leaves in **CROCK-POT**® slow cooker; stir to blend. Cover; cook on LOW 8 to 10 hours.

3. Stir in barbecue sauce. Cover; cook on LOW 1 hour or until heated through. Remove and discard bay leaves.

*To quick soak beans, place beans in large saucepan. Cover with water. Bring to a boil over high heat. Boil 2 minutes. Remove from heat; let soak, covered, 1 hour.

spinach artichoke gratin

Makes 6 servings

  2 cups (16 ounces) cottage cheese
  2 eggs
4½ tablespoons grated Parmesan cheese, divided
  1 tablespoon lemon juice
  ⅛ teaspoon ground nutmeg
  ⅛ teaspoon black pepper
  2 packages (10 ounces *each*) frozen chopped spinach, thawed and squeezed dry
  ⅓ cup thinly sliced green onions
  1 package (10 ounces) frozen artichoke hearts, thawed and halved

1. Add cottage cheese, eggs, 3 tablespoons Parmesan cheese, lemon juice, nutmeg and pepper to food processor or blender; process until smooth.

2. Coat inside of **CROCK-POT®** slow cooker with nonstick cooking spray. Combine spinach, cottage cheese mixture and green onions in large bowl. Spread half of mixture in **CROCK-POT®** slow cooker.

3. Pat artichoke halves dry with paper towels. Place in single layer over spinach mixture. Sprinkle with remaining 1½ tablespoons Parmesan cheese; cover with remaining spinach mixture. Cover with lid slightly ajar to allow excess moisture to escape. Cover; cook on LOW 3 to 3½ hours or on HIGH 2 to 2½ hours.

curried lentils with fruit

Makes 6 servings

  5 cups water
1½ cups dried brown lentils, rinsed and sorted
  1 Granny Smith apple, chopped, plus additional for garnish
  ¼ cup golden raisins
  ¼ cup lemon yogurt
  1 teaspoon salt
  1 teaspoon curry powder

1. Combine water, lentils, 1 chopped apple and raisins in **CROCK-POT®** slow cooker; stir to blend. Cover; cook on LOW 8 to 9 hours or until most liquid is absorbed.

2. Remove lentil mixture to large bowl; stir in yogurt, salt and curry powder until blended. Garnish with additional apple.

cheesy mashed potato casserole

Makes 10 to 12 servings

  4 pounds Yukon Gold potatoes, cut into 1-inch pieces
  2 cups vegetable broth
  3 tablespoons unsalted butter, cubed
  ½ cup milk, heated
  ⅓ cup sour cream
  2 cups (8 ounces) shredded sharp Cheddar cheese,
    plus additional for garnish
  ½ teaspoon salt
  ¼ teaspoon black pepper

1. Coat inside of **CROCK-POT®** slow cooker with nonstick cooking spray. Add potatoes and broth. Dot with butter. Cover; cook on LOW 4½ to 5 hours or until potatoes are very tender.

2. Mash potatoes with potato masher; stir in milk, sour cream, 2 cups cheese, salt and pepper until cheese is melted. Garnish with additional cheese.

curried lentils with fruit

quinoa and vegetable medley

Makes 6 servings

2 medium sweet potatoes, cut into ½-inch-thick slices
1 medium eggplant, cut into ½-inch cubes
1 large green bell pepper, sliced
1 medium tomato, cut into wedges
1 small onion, cut into wedges
½ teaspoon salt
¼ teaspoon ground red pepper
¼ teaspoon black pepper
1 cup uncooked quinoa
2 cups vegetable broth
2 cloves garlic, minced
½ teaspoon dried thyme
¼ teaspoon dried marjoram

1. Coat inside of **CROCK-POT**® slow cooker with nonstick cooking spray. Combine potatoes, eggplant, bell pepper, tomato, onion, salt, ground red pepper and black pepper in **CROCK-POT**® slow cooker; toss to coat.

2. Place quinoa in strainer; rinse well. Add quinoa to vegetable mixture in **CROCK-POT**® slow cooker. Stir in broth, garlic, thyme and marjoram. Cover; cook on LOW 5 hours or on HIGH 2½ hours or until broth is absorbed.

collard greens

Makes 12 servings

- 1 tablespoon olive oil
- 3 turkey necks
- 5 bunches collard greens, stemmed and chopped
- 5 cups chicken broth
- 1 small onion, chopped
- 2 cloves garlic, minced
- 1 tablespoon apple cider vinegar
- 1 teaspoon sugar
  Salt and black pepper
  Red pepper flakes (optional)

1. Heat oil in large skillet over medium-high heat. Add turkey necks; cook and stir 3 to 5 minutes or until brown.

2. Combine turkey necks, collard greens, broth, onion and garlic in **CROCK-POT**® slow cooker; stir to blend. Cover; cook on LOW 5 to 6 hours. Remove and discard turkey necks. Stir in vinegar, sugar, salt, black pepper and red pepper flakes, if desired.

beets in spicy mustard sauce

Makes 4 servings

- 3 pounds beets, peeled, halved and cut into ½-inch slices
- ¼ cup sour cream
- 2 tablespoons spicy brown mustard
- 2 teaspoons lemon juice
- 2 cloves garlic, minced
- ¼ teaspoon black pepper
- ⅛ teaspoon dried thyme

1. Place beets in **CROCK-POT**® slow cooker. Add enough water to cover by 1 inch. Cover; cook on LOW 7 to 8 hours.

2. Combine sour cream, mustard, lemon juice, garlic, pepper and thyme in small bowl; stir to blend. Spoon over beets; toss to coat. Cover; cook on LOW 15 minutes.

collard greens

sweet-sour cabbage with apples and caraway seeds

Makes 6 servings

- 4 cups shredded red cabbage
- 1 large tart apple, peeled, cored and cut crosswise into ¼-inch-thick slices
- ¼ cup packed light brown sugar
- ¼ cup water
- ¼ cup cider vinegar
- ½ teaspoon salt
- ¼ teaspoon caraway seeds
  Dash black pepper

Combine cabbage, apple, brown sugar, water, vinegar, salt, caraway seeds and pepper in **CROCK-POT®** slow cooker; stir to blend. Cover; cook on LOW 2½ to 3 hours.

sweet potato and pecan casserole

Makes 6 to 8 servings

- 1 can (40 ounces) sweet potatoes, drained and mashed
- ½ cup apple juice
- ⅓ cup plus 2 tablespoons butter, melted and divided
- ½ teaspoon salt
- ½ teaspoon ground cinnamon
- ¼ teaspoon black pepper
- 2 eggs, beaten
- ⅓ cup chopped pecans
- ⅓ cup packed brown sugar
- 2 tablespoons all-purpose flour

1. Combine potatoes, apple juice, ⅓ cup butter, salt, cinnamon and pepper in large bowl; beat in eggs. Pour mixture into **CROCK-POT®** slow cooker.

2. Combine pecans, brown sugar, flour and remaining 2 tablespoons butter in small bowl; stir to blend. Spread over sweet potatoes. Cover; cook on HIGH 3 to 4 hours.

sweet-sour cabbage with apples
and caraway seeds

sunshine squash

Makes 6 to 8 servings

 1 butternut squash (about 2 pounds), seeded and diced
 1 can (about 15 ounces) corn, drained
 1 can (about 14 ounces) diced tomatoes
 1 onion, coarsely chopped
 1 green bell pepper, cut into 1-inch pieces
 ½ cup chicken broth
 1 mild green chile, coarsely chopped
 1 clove garlic, minced
 ½ teaspoon salt
 ¼ teaspoon black pepper
 1 tablespoon plus 1½ teaspoons tomato paste

1. Combine squash, corn, tomatoes, onion, bell pepper, broth, green chile, garlic, salt and black pepper in **CROCK-POT**® slow cooker; stir to blend. Cover; cook on LOW 6 hours.

2. Remove about ¼ cup cooking liquid. Stir liquid and tomato paste in small bowl; whisk mixture into **CROCK-POT**® slow cooker. Cover; cook on LOW 30 minutes or until mixture is slightly thickened and heated through.

escalloped corn

Makes 6 servings

2 tablespoons butter
½ cup chopped onion
3 tablespoons all-purpose flour
1 cup milk
4 cups frozen corn, divided
½ teaspoon salt
½ teaspoon dried thyme
¼ teaspoon black pepper
⅛ teaspoon ground nutmeg
  Sprigs fresh thyme (optional)

1. Melt butter in medium saucepan over medium heat. Add onion; cook and stir 5 minutes or until tender. Add flour; cook and stir 1 minute. Stir in milk. Bring to a boil; cook and stir 1 minute or until thickened.

2. Process 2 cups corn in food processor or blender until coarsely chopped. Combine milk mixture, chopped and remaining whole corn, salt, dried thyme, pepper and nutmeg in **CROCK-POT**® slow cooker; stir to blend.

3. Cover; cook on LOW 3½ to 4 hours or until mixture is bubbly around edge. Garnish with fresh thyme.

coconut-lime sweet potatoes with walnuts

Makes 8 servings

2½ pounds sweet potatoes, cut into 1-inch pieces

  8 ounces shredded carrots

  ¾ cup shredded coconut, toasted and divided*

  1 tablespoon unsalted butter, melted

  3 tablespoons sugar

  ½ teaspoon salt

  ⅓ cup walnuts, toasted, coarsely chopped and divided**

  2 teaspoons grated lime peel

To toast coconut, spread evenly on ungreased baking sheet. Toast in preheated 350°F oven 5 to 7 minutes or until light golden brown, stirring occasionally.

**To toast walnuts, spread in single layer in small skillet. Cook and stir over medium heat 1 to 2 minutes or until nuts are lightly browned.*

1. Combine potatoes, carrots, ½ cup coconut, butter, sugar and salt in **CROCK-POT**® slow cooker. Cover; cook on LOW 5 to 6 hours. Remove to large bowl.

2. Mash potatoes with potato masher. Stir in 3 tablespoons walnuts and lime peel. Sprinkle with remaining walnuts and toasted coconut.

braised beets with cranberries

Makes 6 to 8 servings

2½ pounds medium beets, peeled and cut into wedges
 1 cup cranberry juice
 ½ cup sweetened dried cranberries
 2 tablespoons quick-cooking tapioca
 2 tablespoons butter, cubed
 2 tablespoons honey
 ½ teaspoon salt
 ⅓ cup crumbled blue cheese (optional)
   Orange peel, thinly sliced (optional)

1. Combine beets, cranberry juice, cranberries, tapioca, butter, honey and salt in **CROCK-POT**® slow cooker; stir to blend. Cover; cook on LOW 7 to 8 hours.

2. Remove beets to large serving bowl using slotted spoon. Pour half of cooking liquid over beets. Garnish with blue cheese and orange peel.

cauliflower mash

Makes 6 servings

 2 heads cauliflower (8 cups florets)
 1 tablespoon butter
 1 tablespoon half-and-half or whole milk
   Salt
   Sprigs fresh Italian parsley (optional)

1. Arrange cauliflower in **CROCK-POT**® slow cooker; add enough water to fill **CROCK-POT**® slow cooker about 2 inches. Cover; cook on LOW 5 to 6 hours. Drain well.

2. Place cooked cauliflower in food processor or blender; process until almost smooth. Add butter; process until smooth. Add half-and-half as needed to reach desired consistency. Season with salt. Garnish with parsley.

braised beets with cranberries

lemon and tangerine glazed carrots

Makes 10 to 12 servings

6 cups sliced carrots
1½ cups apple juice
6 tablespoons butter
¼ cup packed brown sugar
2 tablespoons grated lemon peel
2 tablespoons grated tangerine peel
½ teaspoon salt
   Fresh Italian parsley, chopped (optional)

Combine carrots, apple juice, butter, brown sugar, lemon peel, tangerine peel and salt in **CROCK-POT**® slow cooker; stir to blend. Cover; cook on LOW 4 to 5 hours or on HIGH 1 to 3 hours. Garnish with parsley.

gratin potatoes with asiago cheese

Makes 4 to 6 servings

6 slices bacon, cut into 1-inch pieces
6 medium baking potatoes, thinly sliced
½ cup grated Asiago cheese
   Salt and black pepper
1½ cups whipping cream

1. Heat large skillet over medium heat. Add bacon; cook and stir until crisp. Remove to paper towel-lined plate using slotted spoon.

2. Pour bacon drippings into **CROCK-POT**® slow cooker. Layer one fourth of potatoes on bottom of **CROCK-POT**® slow cooker. Sprinkle one fourth of bacon over potatoes and top with one fourth of cheese. Season with salt and pepper.

3. Repeat layers three times. Pour cream over all. Cover; cook on LOW 7 to 9 hours or on HIGH 5 to 6 hours.

lemon and tangerine glazed carrots

barley risotto with fennel

Makes 6 servings

 1 medium fennel bulb, cored and finely diced (about ½ cup)
 1 cup uncooked pearl barley
 1 carrot, finely chopped
 1 shallot, finely chopped
 2 teaspoons ground fennel seed
 1 clove garlic, minced
 1 container (32 ounces) chicken broth
 1 cup water
1½ cups frozen cut green beans
 ½ cup grated Parmesan cheese
 1 tablespoon grated lemon peel
 1 teaspoon black pepper

1. Coat inside of **CROCK-POT®** slow cooker with nonstick cooking spray. Combine diced fennel, barley, carrot, shallot, ground fennel and garlic in **CROCK-POT®** slow cooker; stir to blend. Pour in broth and water. Cover; cook on HIGH 3 hours or until barley is thick and creamy.

2. Turn off heat. Stir in green beans, cheese, lemon peel and pepper. (If risotto appears dry, stir in a few tablespoons of additional water.)

parmesan potato wedges

Makes 6 servings

- 2 pounds red potatoes, cut into ½-inch wedges
- ¼ cup finely chopped yellow onion
- 1½ teaspoons dried oregano
- ½ teaspoon salt
- ¼ teaspoon black pepper
- 2 tablespoons butter, cubed
- ¼ cup grated Parmesan cheese

Layer potatoes, onion, oregano, salt, pepper and butter in **CROCK-POT®** slow cooker. Cover; cook on HIGH 4 hours. Remove potatoes to large serving platter; sprinkle with cheese.